WARS

Revolution and Restitution

Poems & Paintings
by J. A. Moss

First published in 2021
by AZILOTH BOOKS

British Library Cataloguing in Publication Data
A catalogue record for this book is available from the British Library:

978-1-913751-16-6

Cover illustration: *Victims of War*, oil painting by J. A. Moss, c. 1970.

DEDICATION

Dedicated to a loving and caring mother who embodied all the values with which 'capital' is not concerned. Who laboured throughout her life to promote and support the wellbeing of six daughters, one son and many others with kindness and sympathy. And to parents everywhere who nurture, love, hope and care.

CONTENTS

PREFACE

At the age of nineteen when studying painting at the Royal College of Art, I decided to reject the idea of non-representational non-objective art and return to visual and natural sources for the basis of my work: portraiture, landscapes, still life objects, to express the beauty of the world which is infinite. Also, as the cover of this book reveals, the suffering of humanity.

In 1993 my mother died and in grief I wrote these tributes.

Because of terrible crimes against the survival of people and the planet it is imperative that we bring to an end the inequality of class and wealth.

J. A. Moss,
November, 2021
Cumbria, U.K.

REPRODUCTION

The fragile pink of the wild rose grows, to glowing sturdy red
The hardened wombs gold seeds tight stacked within its pregnant head
By colour, shine, bright eye attract, be flown and thereby spread

Pendant snowdrop touched with green, squared, swollen pockets fall
Where it stands to colonise and build a solid wall
Of blades and shoots from tiny bulbs light gleaming on the soil

Thistle's green and purple spike becomes the softest crown
The silken threads' fine, feathery, fronds float far to settle down
And firmly spread a sharp star shape, tight set upon the ground

Explosive energy of many yellow dandelions
Volcanically erupt to burst a million golden suns
And lift upturned their opening face to the life giving one
All quickly change to dusty spheres, small moons, dry, silvery
Disperse suspended in the air that more bright suns may be

All is nature's power, her forms contain within
The laws of re-creation great the life force given
Limitless the chances for life to re-exist
That all may live and die, yet the same form persists.

VERGES IN SUMMER – BIRTH

Shoulder high the verges of mix-ed flowers bright
Their varied colour merges suffused with brilliant light

Meadowsweet's cream crumbly blossom 'gainst the purple vetch
Swathes of ghost green bedstraw luminously stretch
Sharp spiked tough bold thistle pushes high its head
Lank leaf of rusty sorrel within the green shows red

Harebells blue bellflowers tremble in the grass
Whose feathery seeds show flaxen or sweetest soft pink mass
Yellow centred daisies display their virgin petals
Near tall tapering towers of stalwart stinging nettles

Platters of sturdy hogweed above all others stand
Tempting iridescent flies to cease their flight and land.
In hedge with curving fingers blond honeysuckle grows
Rambling high abundantly beside the wild pink rose.

Probing climbing bindweeds tightening tendrils twine
Round and up for fleshy cup to utilise a spine.
Sprouting with full vigour light creamy coronets
Lush elder bush is smothered by frothy flowerets.

Clumps of strong , stout ragwort stiffly stand below
Golden in the sunshine dazzlingly they glow.
In light against a background of verdant foliage
A moving dappled mass of leaves – a rich, dark curtilage .

To these fine flowering forms the bare black soil gives birth
Producing and revealing the fecundity of Earth.

14

GLEN AFFRIC

A winding road accompanies glen's river
Whose deepening darks contrast with glistening silver
Up from the verge rocks rise, rose pink, cool blue
Pale yellow, gold and greys of varied hue
Reflecting light their substance crystalline
Each tiny facet glitters diamantine
Plants in profusion grow luxuriantly
Filling each space with their fecundity
Stout saplings in the fissures generate
Sweet flowers on the rock face propagate
        Abundantly brash bracken spreads and smothers
Knee high greens the hillside, thwarting others
Autumn changes covered mountain slope
Transforms it to a bright kaleidoscope
Auburn, orange, crimson, lemon, gold
Emerald, carmine, fiery scarlet bold
Torrential rain turns trunks of trees to black
Black peat the soaking soil along the track
In brilliant blue white castle clouds float by
Purple mountains dominate the sky
        Ferns, plump mosses cushion every stone
On rocks blithe water slips from silk to foam
Fish split the gleaming surface to catch flies
Concentric circles spread to their demise
A heavy swollen cloud gloomily glowers
Hurling straight to earth its twinkling showers
Trickling down rough rocky mountainside
Rivulets combine to broaden wide
Approaching fast a narrow precipice
Rushing past a plateau to abyss
A frantic froth of water falls the chasm
Each droplet bouncing rock to rock in spasm
To plunge the tranquil river far below
And round the verdant islands smoothly flow

Eddying winds in birch and alder stirs
Their myriad leaves; sharp needles of the firs
Lichens, mosses, pad strong limbs of trees
Starry flowers support bold probing bees
Sunlight glows where trees stand far apart
Dragonflies glint fiercely as they dart
Swarms of dancing insects forma ball
Fluttering altogether rise and fall
Smart butterflies flit down to dry their wings
Enchanting thrush in branches loudly sings
Last year's leaves fill spaces underfoot
Round the mossy trunks protruding root
And turning forest's green to earthy red
Make the woodland ground a fertile bed
Intent on journey with full concentration
Black beetle staggers on to destination
A crumbling cottage empty by the road
Within its dampness croak the frog and toad
Bilberries blue, mauve heathers cover ground
Beside each other joined in rounded mound
A crouching hare in undergrowth shows fear
Haloes of light frame each long wary ear
Slender legged deer to safety bound
The antlered head with dignity turns round
Wide winged eagle slowly circles high
Surveying rodents' land with piercing eye
Below on mountainside the road ascends
By creviced rocks above tree tops the incline bends
Skirting a sharp uneven steep gradine
Crowning the tree filled slopes of deep ravine
To reach a sparkling loch of lustrous shine
Broken by rich islands dark with pine
Towards the west majestic mountains rise
O'erlapping in the distance glimmering skies

Oh! Glorious, glorious is the sight of these
Space, light, mountains, water, rocks and trees.

SLAUGHTERED TREES

Ah! Trees majestic beauty, of root, of trunk, of crown
Men with axe and chainsaw, with labour cut you down
Field by field extending, their flattened forms abound
Round their edge one tree or hedge, is left from woodland ground

Oh! mighty Beech, flow'rd Chestnut, fine Birch, tall Lime, giant Oak
Full Sycamore, pure Ash tree turned to fire's dark smoke
Sliced or split to silvered shapes, a box or boundary make
Or paltry post, their beauty lost, their curves straightened stake

Great leafy crown, high fluttering dome, a rich light flickering green
Almighty trunk, with rising sap from earth through roots unseen
Housing life of nesting, of resting crawling creatures
The living leaf, the burgeoning limb, a mass of complex features

Protruding in the hedgerow, a shortened stump fast dies
On the roadside, on its side, denuded trunk last lies
Dragged by chain, sawn branchless, its tortured shape distorted
Reduced from noble upright, horizontally transported

Monsters with crude chain between, rupture, rip and grind
Dragging, tearing, scraping, leaving, severed life behind
Cathedrals for heart piercing song, rain forest gone, deserted
Richness burnt to charcoal, to barrenness converted

Empty fields from nibbling, close cropped grass pervading
Nipped, the trees young opening shoots, with voracious raiding
Shorn rough tufted hillside, its surface smooth, cut short
Curving canopies of trees, destroyed, become as naught

On smooth tree felled mountainside, rivulets rush down
Tumbling, twisting, bubbling, forcing lower land to drown
Swollen rivers, lakes on fields, caused from forests slaughter
House and street, under meet, submerged by seeping water

Miles of murky moorland, kept to murder birds
Within low heather hiding the beater's stick disturbs
To fly with fear into the air as targets shot for pleasure
Bagged and bragged about and hung, counted in full measure

Replacing forests, cities: of steel, cement, glass, brick
Engulfing acres fusing, a grey crustacean thick
Scab of blocks repeating, crammed close to spread far wide
Forest crushed by roads and walls, beneath hard stone has died

A hill remains whose rising slopes, are smothered by dense trees
Rough roaming winds rush through and ripple rounded canopies
Intoxicating blue beneath, the mind enraptured, drunk
By vivid colour wrapping round a glowing mossy trunk

Bluebells! bells of blue emerge delighting eye and head
Feet are sunk into the depth of flowers in their bed
Above, a bursting canopy of fragile leaves uncoil

Each tree, lush, thick laden with vibrant leaves of green
Dense mass of swaying splendour, profuse enchanting screen
Luxuriant magnificence, abundant grand design
Prolific their virility, divine, supreme, sublime

Each twig with fulsome flowers, opening delight
Attracting by their powers, the bee in tireless flight
To penetrate, to pollinate, to propagate each seed
Bountifully fertile, fulfilling Nature's need

Sharp edged dusky shadows cool summers sultry heat
A golden light, blinding bright, a dappled sunlit streak
In stripes and patches of sun's warmth dancing insects play
Within dark rows clear sunlight glows and shows the verdant way

Brilliant jewelled trees rich red, autumnal amber crown
Of dying, falling, rustling, leaves, slowly turning brown
The tree they shared, one by one, they leave bereft to go
Wafting down to settle, to rest, to rot below

Enriching for trees swollen seed a full sustaining bed
Supporting new existence nourished by leaves dead
For searching shoot of stem or root striving deep or higher
Their sturdy growth created by Sun's immortal fire

Fearful rage, harsh hurling storm, through dark tumultuous sky
Then silence... floating snowflakes, building bulk up high
Each twig, each branch, soft covered, their winter shape reformed
Quiet, stilled, each space white filled, by snow, woodland transformed

Heaven! such heaven as ever is, is here, is down on Earth
Above in space, massed brilliant clouds, trees canopy traverse
Who would? How could? this heaven, the axe and fire disperse
Create denuded landscape, on Nature leave their curse

A crime! a crime against the world, against its pulse, its breathing
A crime against the atmosphere, against the earth of seething
Life... its great variety, its rich diversity
Restore the forests, plant new trees, for all posterity

THE BARE HILLS

Sharp edged bones of bare hills show through denuded soil
Gone are glorious woodlands from centuries of toil
With axe with cutting with burning and felling of forests of trees
Trunks and branches have disappeared and gone are the canopy's leaves.

The land is shaped and parcelled its flattened fields are bare
Within enclosing boundaries no foot must venture there
A few trees left now banished to skirt the pressured edge
Their high imposing majesty reduced to a low hedge.

Wind tossed bright sweet flowers made varied coloured land
Are now reduced to verges to flower a narrow band
Where sheep and heavy cattle crop the children cannot play
The rest is covered streets of stone or roads or motorway.

One narrow footpath given, along the edge of field
In order to protect the land to give the utmost yield
In rooms, in schools, in offices, confined imprisoned sigh
Through dust on sunny windows stare out to view the sky

Beyond, the world pulsates with life and throbs with light and sound
Rushing water, all the plants erupting in the ground
Over again and over the pressured soil must give
Throughout the varied seasons the pressured crop must live.

Upon the treeless hillside rain's water penetrates
The oozing slippery rootless earth, a murder perpetrates
Sweeping all before it depriving all of breath
Light and beauty blotted out in darkened muddy death.

I long with intense feeling that soon will be restored
Full glory of rich foliage magnificence of wood
The undulating hillside with sharpened silhouette
Would be part covered over by growing forms which met.

In one abundant flowering, gold green of solid Oak
Festoons of leaves from Beech and Lime, bulging woods to cloak
And curve and cover, create again rich land
For nesting birds to hover, below the nurturing band.

Of fallen leaves in undergrowth, a dark sustaining loam
A carpet of thick foliage with varied colour shown
White heads of Garlic, bells of blue, yellow petal bright
Sweet scented air, winds movement, sunshine's flickering light.

Epilogue

No more the bare cropped field and hill
For murdered beast, more beast to fill
The fresh young calf, so newly born
From swollen udders rudely torn
The grieving cow, the murdered lamb
Slaughtered all, *ad nauseam*
The rich soil forced and over sprayed
A flowerless crop throughout displayed
If hill and field with flowers be filled
And plants for food, no beast be killed
Trees in abundance spread the earth
An enriched soil gives back their birth
For those confined and trapped within
A freer life might then begin.

BALLAD OF THE HIGHLAND CLEARANCES

The greedy Duke and rich Duchess
Made money from clan's homelessness
To them perfidious clan chieftain
Sold green glen and high mountain.
They would then the land 'improve'
If they could but the clan remove
To lease high land for wool from sheep
The revenue which they would keep.
Others from the lowlands came
To buy seized land and stake their claim
Laws were passed and orders given
Clansmen from their land be driven.

Grim factor came with written word
Soldiers with their fire and sword
And brutally removed from glen
Babies, children, women, men
Infirm were dragged, undignified
To freeze on cold and wet hillside
Soldiers burnt their crops and crofts
Soldiers torched their walls and lofts
Destroyed their tools, laid waste their home
Forced them dispossessed to roam
To try to find another place
Across the world's unfriendly face.

Ranged against the Highlanders
Were usurping landowners
Written word of litigation
Reverend with 'god's' castigation
Sheriff, factor, unjust law
Police, batons, swords of war
Rent exacting tacksman tough
Absconding chief with wealth enough
For profit, gain, great was the price
The crofters paid with sacrifice
From their land they were evicted
And with violence inflicted.

The women laughed defiantly
And bravely faced the soldiery
Tore the papers straight across
Could not comprehend their loss
Resistance quiet did not prevent
Attack hostile and violent
Broken bodies hurled around
Kicked and trampled into ground
Muddied bloodied against stone
From bridge to icy water thrown
Victims of greed's heartlessness
Were thus forced out to homelessness.

Severe the suffering and distress
Felt by those made powerless
For they knew not where to go
To escape wild wind and snow
Locked from church, they huddled all
Shivering against its wall
Inscribed its window with their name
To show that they to life had claim
Hunger came and poverty
As others claimed their property
Reduced to wretched hopelessness
Were those with clear blamelessness

Crushed in ship's small darkened hold
Were displaced clans young and old
People who had not before
Ever left loch land and shore
But lived in green and rivered glen
As rough and independent men
Built small townships stony croft
Worked fine soil where rich and soft
Life was hard and they were poor
Rent they paid and burdens bore
Animals their croft would share
Filling dense dark smoky air

Outside pure air the valley green
Above, majestic mountains seen
Foaming waters rushed down by
Their shelter from a cloud filled sky
Their life was full of industry
From purposeful necessity
A chieftain did their minds inspire
The clan united their life's fire
Until the land for sheep was sold
And their life bartered for cheap gold
And their united place was shattered
And they across the world were scattered.

Now lush glens and mountains steep
Are scoured by herds of cropping sheep
Trees which try to send up shoots
Are nibbled constantly to roots
Ruined croft, now craggy mound
Of stones rough tumbled on waste ground
Silent glens without the toil
Of clansmen tilling enriched soil
A people gone, banished, dispersed
Forced to leave by law coerced
Forced by fire, by sword to sever
And part from their high land for ever.

Killing Grounds

Bleak moors created for the cover
For shooting pheasant, grouse and plover
Hare and fox pursued to death
Satisfy with their last breath
Spawning salmon leaping, thrilling
Give men purpose in their killing
Deer are hounded, stalked and shot
Massacred and then forgot
All face death of little reason
As war against their life's in season
From those whose wealth controls the bridle
Death, destruction, thrill's the idle.

PERMANENTLY STILL

The Duke has little right to stand
In stone, high on the hill
For he stole the clansmen's land
Now permanently still

Piles of stones lie heaped
Down below the hill
Remains of homes removed
Now permanently still

Deadly conifers forlorn
Blanketing the hill
Ugly, dense and uniform
Permanently still

Empty frames of pylons
Winding round the hill
Resting, standing skeletons
Permanently still

The glen lies quiet, deserted
And sheep high on the hill
Denude the land, converted
To be permanently still.

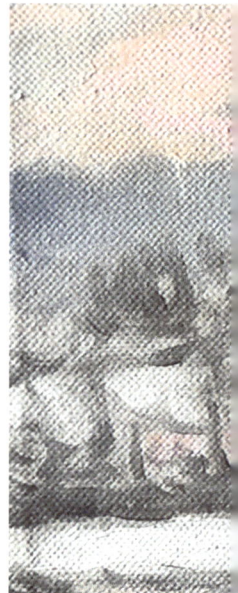

MURDER AND CANNIBALISM

The cow, the bull, the little calf
Are disembowelled, cut in half
Further sliced and spliced and diced
Packaged into size and priced
For cooking, roasting, baking, stewing
Placed on plates for people's chewing

The pig will suffer the same fate
Sliced as bacon on a plate.
So the chicken, duck and swan
So the sheep and lamb are gone
In their billions all are slaughtered
Bled and hung and drawn and quartered.

Animal eats animal
We are omnivore
We two legged ones do eat
Those that run on four
But we have conscience to enable
Rejection of the execrable
And change from meat to vegetable.

DESTRUCTION, PERSECUTION AND CREATION

Where have wild flowers gone, dense canopies of trees?
Barren the fields where there are none, empty as stony screes
In bounded land sheep nibbled, flower's hue has waned
Imbalance and in quantity a mono-crop sustained
Ancient forests sunk below have turned to brittle coal
Now tunnelled, hacked and harvested by burrowing human mole
Rich the viscous oil pumped high, draining earth's black blood
Turning to blackening fumes and dust rare residue of wood
Huge cities rise as blocks thrown high, smothering lost soil
Filled with teeming energy and frantic human toil
With money as a life blood, suffusing every vein
Causing wars of nations for suppos-ed gain
Intense the fierce destruction, gross the weapons made
With purposeful direction, creation retrograde

Within restricting boundaries, national barriers real
Hatred of the other gives power to kill and steal
To persecute, annihilate, destroy in utmost pain
With callousness, with carelessness, are other people slain
Calculated, concentrated, formed in squares of order
Are soldiers of the rulers, prepared for war and murder
With tank, with gun, with bomb, the caesarean aeroplane
Discharges obscene offspring to fall as killing rain
Imaginary hell becomes, reality created
As we and where we dwell are both obliterated
Oil and coal and metal , with fire of fierce explosion
Misuse of earth's resources causing chaos and confusion
Ending life for millions in bravery and fear
An end in mud and blood and dust of young life purchased dear

Creating wealth for profiteers the mass of people strive
And with patience struggle, desiring to survive
In wars between the rulers is each nation shaken
With arrogant conscription, is each person taken
Organised into a force, submit to every order
Transported far to unknown lands as a cruel marauder
Against opposing people the soldiers guns are turned
Innocence is slaughtered, cities whole are burned
No quarrel soldiers have with those they're forced to slay
The conquest is not for them, though they cause affray

Populations suffer in brutal bloody war
Struggle, strive, accepting lies still remaining poor
Anger, then resistance among the people grows
With powerful persistence, revolution overthrows

From war's ash arises a people traumatized
Yet turning dust and chaos, to order, civilized
In ruined shattered cities are buildings new remade
The pummelled soil reformed, new foundations laid
Wounded yet the old form of money still survives
Casting poverty's sad shape, blanketing new lives
It's past pompous certainty, shaken to the core
Its oppressive empires to exist no more
Its failing architecture supposed high success
Reflected in high towers, high blocks to impress
Ramshackle little shanties which hug the mud below
Filled with struggling poverty and energy to grow
Iniquity of rulers, with force, try to prevail
Against the firm endurance their unjust wars do fail

Crumbling fast around us, money's fortress falls
Jagged cracks to ground lay bare, decimated walls
Each stone in succession slipping from its place
The edifice collapsing, plunging in disgrace
Arms by arms are lifted, with purpose to oppose
Oppressed in thought uplifted, inspired to expose
Rising from the ruins may be a fairer state
With new struggles forming to organize its fate
For wealthy towers of steel and glass, new destiny be found
Shabby shacks of shanties erased from putrid ground
Freed from tyranny of wealth or dearth of sustenance
Equality and Liberty with Fraternity advance
Released from bloody war and pain filled poverty
All rise in strength, free from stain, restored humanity

WORKERS AND DRONES

The honey bee all summer long
Back and forth wings with her song
Unceasing her activity
Creating gold divinity
Sun-filled, sweet viscosity
Building shaped complexity
Combs with her dexterity
Cleaning, feeding, tending young
With wings, antennae, body, tongue
Collecting, filling, enriching hive
Enabling countless to survive
The flower, the tree, to pollinate
Promoting plants to germinate
And verdant forests generate

Within the hive the queen lives long
Producing a united throng
A swarm which can be spooned from tree
And housed in hives dark mystery
Of workers, nymphs, princesses, drones
In waxen cells each one entombed
To emerge a bright new bee
Begin, again, maintain, fly free
The princess buzzes angrily
Stings in cell her sister rivals
Ensuring thus her own survival
To become the single one
To fly high towards the sun
To create a great new swarm

In splendid coloured plumery
Live burnished drones in finery
Many will the queen produce
Only one to reproduce
The princess in her maiden flight
Attracts all drones to match her height
The beauty of her maiden scent
Excites with sweetest enchantment
Soaring high and ever higher
Towards bright sun does she aspire

31

Followed by the drones desire
To impregnate and expire
In azure blue, above, unseen
To be the being who makes new queen
In ecstatic single flight
The entwined pair reach great height
In beauty and in ecstasy
He falls wounded - mortally
His entrails deeply are embedded
In the princess, newly wedded
Descending, landing, to be seen
To show entrails, to be queen
Welcomed back into the hive
Feted, nurtured, to provide
New young who fill waxen cell
Emerge, collect from flower's well
Clear nectar, honey's gold create
Thus the world to propagate

When summer's work is nearly done
And autumn winds cool summer sun
And flowers have changed to vivid fruit
And nectar gone from flowers throat
Then does the busy working bee
Consider life's necessity
The surplus part of a vast hive
At end of summer won't survive
The drones in lazy luxury
Lounging, lax, desultory
Splendid drones with honey fed
Find themselves without a bed
As they return, full of hunger
Meet repellent, full of anger
Those who laboured for so long
Cannot support the useless throng
Decide the hive must now be free
From their inactivity
And covering with vicious stings
Pull off their heads, their legs, their wings
Glorious plumes are rent to dust
In a heap they lie a crust

Of dismembered, shattered glory
A cruel end to their proud story
And so to our society
Full of love and industry
With workers keeping all alive
As honey bees within the hive

Wealth created as bees honey
Is abstraction, riches, money
Unlike the living of the bee
It wreaks of inequality
From industrious labour made
With poverty is overlaid
While bees create rich golden honey
Rich turn life, to gold, to money
To crush subject humanity
They manufacture weaponry
Across the globe they rage and war
Drowning us in blood and gore
Released from their vile tyranny
We could be freed from poverty
Those who commit atrocity
Of wars savage monstrosity
Destroy and kill, oppress and fill
The world with costly weaponry
Must know exploited workers see
Injustice and wars cruelty
Decide their life must now be free
Of ruthless inhumanity
Create a worldwide revolution
Free the earth of wars pollution
Replacing wealth and poverty
With liberty, equality
To those against fraternity
Be warned by fate of drone of bee!

EPILOGUE

Without the bee, we may not see
A world enriched by greenery
Seemingly, her task to be
To propagate each flower and tree
Men build town and city hives
With money making spend their lives
Smother soil with glass and stone
Live as worker or as drone

Fill the world with plastic toys
Pollute the air with fumes and noise
Rushing here, there, everywhere
Each heart weighted down by care
All concerned with money making
All involved in money taking
Some with less, some with more
Becoming rich, remaining poor
Creating myth, producing dearth
From commerce spreading throughout earth
A blight defiling each creation
Forcing war between each nation
No peace will be until the curse
Is lifted from the face of Earth
Then our lives could, as the bee
Nurture life's divinity

WORLD CAPITALISM

Power is in Capital not Kings
Capital has free flight in its wings
Across world continents to multiply
Intangible invisible to human eye
It is not seen here there, or anywhere
Yet permeating everything is everywhere
An abstraction yet with all within kept fast
No one escapes it from the first to last
Things will exist or not according to its laws
Imbalance inequality its mores
Pursues its interests to extend its cause
Produces conflicts and creates its wars

OIL

Conquering brute of Capital opens wide its jaws
Tearing bleeding masses with its sharpened teeth and claws
It swallows with wide greedy gulps the Earth's varied resources
Spewing forth a wealth of "goods" and Wars invading forces

Shimmering in the desert the broad light pipeline winds
Through continents, on rough terrain in long straight solid lines
Within, the viscous oil pulses through the arteries
Dark treasure of past centuries drawn from Earth's cavities

With brute force, with lies, with tanks, they move on in to kill
To violate a nation, to steal the oil and spill
The rich red blood of innocents, for oil is to be sold
And turned from thick black slippery grease to money's shining gold.

WAR

Throughout your life, all day, all night, vile vicious wars have raged
Have hacked and torn and blown apart our most precious babes.
The pressure of one finger lets hell loose upon the world
And fruit of a million sacred wombs is into darkness hurled.
Earth's delicate crust is pitted, denuded of living green
Earth's water cannot quench the pain or drown the anguished scream;
Metal, blood, bone and mud, in scorched disharmony
Anger, fear, distrust, despair oppose your living testimony

THEY TURN THE TOWNS TO TOMBS

Every town, every village, owns a monument with names
Showing where the young were pillaged, forced to fight for others aims
Torn from life of air and sunlight, to the mud of Ypres and Mons
Shattered by the cracking gunfight, were young fathers, lovers, sons

Writhing horses, useless flailing, carts and cannon deep in mud
Lice filled clothing, rat infested, rotting bodies steeped in blood
Bandage bound round blinded sockets, stumbling foot and fumbling hand
Mud caked, blood soaked heaps on stretchers, murdered for a clod of land

––––––––––––––––

For this great grisly purpose were youthful bodies torn
Forced from families to fight, conform in uniform
To do as bidden, feelings hidden, take another's life
Losing hope and happiness, to misery and strife

Berated, marched and brutalised, to trample under boot
With metal bayonet and gun, a million bullets shoot
To pierce the living lung or leg or arm or heart or head
The innocent or 'enemy' to leave a million dead

Each vivid life was stolen and strewn into the grave
Wasting thoughts complexity to be unthinking slave
Made to think that crime committed was no crime at all
Praised as noble heroes, with medals at their fall

Criminal the guilty men who sent them off to war
Who took them young, forced on them gun and knife to kill far 1
Made them dig their grave, a trench, for concentrated slaughter
As targets crouching to avoid flying shell and mortar

In shivering fear, cold, hungry, tired, in dark and rain
Deafened by explosives, delivering death or pain
Some sick with shaking shell shock, cowed by callous carnage
Were hooded, tied to stake and shot, for showing 'lack of courage'

Cruel the guilty men who send an army off to fight
To aim to maim the enemy, extinguishing their light

Ooze blood rich red or bodies dead, a precious womb did grow
Their flesh torn groans, their shattered bones, their Mother's pain filled woe

Heinous, guilty officers who build a murdering throng
Who hurl abuse and make them lose all sense of right or wrong
To wound, destroy a living being that they have never seen
With pretence of a defence of Nation' or of "Queen'

Forming armies, making weapons, raising up a national pride
Rolling tanks across with soldiers, armed to teeth to fight world wide
Dispossessing and repressing, arrogantly all despising
Master Race' a 'Chosen People' madness in the mind arising

Patriotism' "Nationalism' divisions of our times
Attacking other peoples, produces wars harsh crimes
Depriving them of life and land, for few to gain wealth's riches
Fighting for the world's resources, turning soil to ditches

Continuous the brutal wars that they do perpetrate
Convincing all that others are full of fearful hate
Commandeering earth's resources, populace enslave
Weapons of relentless forces, causing early grave

Fiendish flowers, roots of wire, triggered touch to spurt
An unexpected reaping of tearing, searing, hurt
Exploding bulb of killing ore, steel seed, sharp iron petal
To gash, rip, slash, through heart, gut, bone, with shredded shards of metal

On upturned ship, tight clinging, to broken hull or mast
Sucked through cold deep water, drowning, sinking fast
Shattered stern and mangled men, on ocean bed to settle
Side by side, devoured, soft flesh, bone and metal

In space, through clouds, in atmosphere, in ethereal light
Roaring metal of machines, rear gunners fatal fight
Hunting, chasing, aiming, with deadly shooting games
Plummeting to earth, to smash, in smoke, on fire, in flames

Hovering helicopter with hostile prying eye
Probing, droning overhead to ominously spy
Releasing harmful cargo to cruelly bequeath
Dismemberment or sudden death on those who are beneath

Piercing planes with booming voice hurtling forth in space
Dropping bursting cluster bombs to brutally efface
Blitzing, strafing, raiding with fierce insanity
Unprovoked aggression toward humanity

Coagulating Napalm, atomic nuclear bombs
Down through air, with raging fire, towns are turned to tombs
Devastation rages, razed blasted masonry
Infernal heat, a people melt, their world a cemetery

Babies, Mothers, Fathers, Young Children, all as one
Unperceiving, are receiving death from falling bomb
And on the ground more murder from vicious soldiery
Recruited from the poor, for war, for slaughter, butchery

Propping up stooge governments, with lies, with arms suppressing
Pouring in rich revenue, for purposely oppressing
Persecuting populace, brutality persisting
Opposing in their fight for life, the brave, inspired, resisting

Hideous wars dictators, their sick obscenity
Vicious, cruel committing their vile atrocity
Torturing, hating, hostile, depraved barbarity
Worldwide the deep infection of war's depravity

Oh wretched war! Oh misery! overthrow its crime
Oppose their force, their wars far worse, to live a fruitful time
Change their wealth, their domination causing war's destruction
Free our lives from guns and knives, their bombs, their vain corruption

The U.S.A. and also the UK have bombed the following countries since 1945 (the end of the second world war: a conflict between capitalist nations of Europe, America and Japan in which millions of people were killed).
China (1945 - 46 & 1950- 53)
Korea (1950 - 53)
Guatemala (1954 - 60)
Indonesia (1958)
Cuba (1959 -60)
Congo (1964)
Peru (1965)
Laos (1964 73)
Vietnam (1961 -73)
N. Ireland (1967- 2006)
Cambodia (1969 - 70)
Guatemala (1967 - 69)
Chile (1971)
Falklands (1982)
Grenada (1983)
Libya (1986)
El Salvador & Nicaragua (all of the 1980's)
Panama (1989)
Iraq (1991 -99)
Sudan (1998)
Afghanistan (1998)
Yugoslavia (1999)
Afghanistan (2002-2)
Iraq (2003-)

Israel with American backing is bombing Palestinians.
Russia has bombed Afghanistan, Chechnya and Syria
Wars persist throughout the world.

WAR 1914-18

When you were budlike flowering
Formed sweetly by nature's hands
Jaws of war were devouring
The youth of many lands

Armies of millions were fashioned, arms in their arms to uphold
Empire then raged against empire and cast their young men in a mould
To kill others at bidding of others, to kill others that they never knew
For others the rifle the knife and the bomb, each other their brothers they slew

From every city town and village, every valley strath and glen
Europe's imperial hand did pillage and gather a harvest of men
With brutal shouts and violence, with threats of punishment dire
They were forced to bayonet and to learn to fire

Forced to give life hardly known, before developed or fully grown
To feel the chilling fear.
Try to be brave and face the grave which they knew was lying near
A deep trench waiting to receive a batch of raw recruits
A massacre of innocents which Pontius Pilate shoots

To smell the stench in the muddy trench of the bloody gore in the mire
With rats, with mice, crawling with lice, scorched and blasted by fire
Squelching through mud, slipping in blood, dismembered corpses trod down
Wounded they'd lie, bloodied they'd die, in a filthy crack in the ground

Like a vein pulsating with blood, viewed under a microscope
Millions of men in a living grave, confined with little hope
Where shrapnel or cruel mortar would cause ghastly wound or blind
Or force them to leave a youthful arm or youthful leg behind

Or be given an order to move out over the top
With the crack of a loud bullet, their precious life would stop
In mud, in rain, in fear, in pain, see no blade of living grass
TO DIE and kill others like themselves for a barbarous ruling class

Those who by good fortune and with great relief returned
Who tried to re-adjust and their former life re-learned
Were not as fully whole as when they first were sent
Suffered sickness in their soul and had their spirits rent.

WORLD WAR II – 1939 to 1945
(55 million murdered)

You to a mother had grown
Again young people were taken, this time they were your own.

The Fascist might of Europe with power to tyrannize
Persecuting others, aimed to de-humanize
From distorted minds of hate came vile depravity
Causing boundless suffering, a great calamity.
How effectively destroy the Jews and suffering poor
And create slave labour for their domination and war?
Established forms, carefully thought, action deliberate
Intolerable intention, to gas and exterminate.
Confined within a fence of wire, bound by ferocity
Were huddled heaps of skin and bone, a grim atrocity
Through the chimneys the fetid smell of bodies cruelly scorched
Emaciated and starving, confined together and torched.
Heaps of flopping corpses were inhumanly bulldozed
Shuffled, scooped to lime pits and uncaringly disposed
Little children fleeing in ships, were sunk by bombs and drowned
Others were buried alive to swell and move the ground.
With anguish, fear and misery, despair, distress and pain
The vulnerable and innocent were forced to war again.

The mighty strength of capital's nation states
Unleashed their weapons with furious, frenzied hate
Through air, on land, above, below the seas
Metal clashed and flashed, denuded the land of trees.
The skies were filled with fighting aeroplanes
Crashing to earth on fire, with smoke and flames
Across the oceans ships sank by the tons
As they blasted death, destruction from their guns.
Cities laboriously built of hand sized stones
Were violently blown to rubble and bones
With fire, explosions, bombs, with guns and smoke
Destructive capital's vicious anger smote
The people of each nation suffered within
As it crushed their bones and burnt their delicate skin
In their millions they all suffered and died
As arrogant war destroyed their life worldwide.

MYTH AND THE ROAD OF BONES

Incarcerated, ingrained with stones
Lie entrapped fine human bones
Buried to increase the load
To build Siberia's solid road
Fruit of twenty million wombs
End as ballast in hard tombs
Where they fell, starved and cold
There they dwell in rigid mould
Condemned by lie, unarmed civilian
To drudge, to die, all twenty million
Abducted, driven as herded cattle
Subjected to machine-gun rattle
Gulags, camps, interrogation
Pain intense from mutilation
Accusation, torture, death
Innocence losing innocent breath
Tyrants vile of ruthless nature

Myth uplifts to lofty stature
Worshipped, favoured, feared, praised
Seen as God on platform raised
Proudly saluting grand processions
Menacing, threatening, vicious weapons
In narrow slits, suspicious eye
Building a mountain of men to spy
Permeating each relation
Destroying hope and aspiration

Inspired the wish, desired the change
From brutal exploitation
Monstrous madness the derange
Of brutal persecution.
As stones are captured, frozen within ice
So lie whole human frames as road infill
Result of hardened hearted caught in vice
All kindly action numbed by unkind will
Unable to express or sympathise

Or give to human suffering relief
Or with clear mind to simply recognize
The agony of all engulfing grief
But carry through a huge iniquity
Against the innocent whose captive state
Make them sad victims of cold cruelty
As necessary beings who relate
To those who persecute and do not see
Greatness, strength, beauty in humanity

However deeply buried are base deeds
Of cruelty by other humans made
With ignorance unfeeling or false creed
Killing fine aspiration by crusade
Into the mind fresh knowledge underscores
Stirring strong courage from clear truth sublime
Of conscience, with opposing hope filled cause
To conquer forcefully corrupting crime
Dethroned are tyrants then, in time erased
All former worship and the high esteem
Downcast, their brutal action, callous, crazed
Striving to restrain th' enduring stream
Of unnamed millions who throughout the Earth
Love, hope and struggle toward noble worth .

Epilogue

Within abundant oceans of Earth's globe
Erupt high mountains on lowlands plateau
Lush teeming forests plentifully robe
Through which sweet veins of pulsing rivers flow
Fertility, profusion, run through all
Rich nature seemingly with constant law
Replaces life by ceaseless rise and fall
Within this beauty rages unjust war
With devastation nations clash for gain
Of wealth, against another ruling class
Cause bloodshed, death, destruction, despair, pain
To subdue, exploit, impoverished mass
And nature, raided, vandalized, impaired
Whose fertile wealth could nurture all if shared

NUCLEAR WEAPONRY

When I was young, aged three or four, a book for me you bought
Hard bound, within its covers a 'magic' world it taught
Of demons, fairies, towers tall
Dark crimes, youth's love which conquers all:
Here then mother is a tale, black as any 1 feel
More bitter, cruel and sad, as it happens to be real.

There was a little devil and unhappy was he
He wasn't doing well at destroying humanity
Then he had an idea: "1 know what to do
Give them gift or maybe one or two
Let them split the atom, a small and powerful form
And from the smallest can the largest soon be born."
The atom then was split and as the devil knew
On the city of Hiroshima and Nagasaki too
In the early morning when they had just awoken
Man then loosed his hell and all heaven's heart was broken
The BURNING, the DESTRUCTION and the SCREAMING PAIN
The AGONY, the SUFFERING, the devil came again
Another gift deliver: "This one is not enough
I will give some more of a similar sort of stuff
The destruction must be bigger and be continuous
A chain reaction which could be completely ruinous
The poisons must pollute the air, the rivers and the sea
And pollute the soil or unhappy I will be
If they can grow their food and drink water fresh and clean
If the world is covered by verdure rich and green."
So to practice once again, to cause the utmost pain
Nuclear bomb explosions grew big and even bigger
Producing barren areas as man released the trigger
The air became polluted and little children died
And many healthy humans were completely horrified
And tiny islands rich with life where shone the sun's bright light
Exploded and underneath the sea and in the deserts gold
More explosions practiced for the agony of the world.
The devil came again "I'll give more and more and more
I must have nuclear installations along every shore
I must have black plutonium to spread throughout the seas
To contaminate and cause cancerous disease

The waste must last for aeons and be indestructible
With certain death contained within each tiny particle
Because it's in their nature to enable them to learn
People make 'mistakes' and many more will burn.
I can be sure that often there will be some awful leaks
And people will be suffering for years and months and weeks
I'll say it's for production of electricity
To warm, and lighten darkness, so that they may see."
The devil grinned and danced and he rubbed his horny hands
As nuclear plants grew rapidly in many different lands
And as the devil planned with his pernicious skill
Man relaxed intense and continuous vigil
The whole deadly plant exploded, its name was Chernobyl
HELL ON EARTH again the poisonous fire and smoke
Erupted into air and across the world did float
The clouds with lethal poison dropped their precious rain
And mountains, rivers, animals, radioactive all became
From Italy's glorious mountains to the northern Lapland plain
The animals and grasses within man's rich food chain.

Now this devil had a wife, she was a devil too
He called her his "trouble and strife" (as many devils do)
She was grey and poisonous, her name Plutonium
One touch from her fatal finger would cause pandemonium
The devil was quite miserable, a deep sigh he did give
"The poisons are not strong enough, people continue to live"
Don't forget your daughter products" this devil wife replied
"Uranium, Caesium, Strontium, which you can put inside
Your 'Trident' which the depth of sea can very easily hide
They can help you pull the trigger if they combine and then implode
Their reaction will be bigger and the whole world could explode
If we have four we'll carry more, sixteen in everyone
Eight separate heads, targeted, we can have some fun."
The devil laughed "You clever wife, that will be a splendid game
To remain in hiding and to set their world aflame
To chase and to appear, to frighten and to scare
To kill them when defenceless and to aim from anywhere"
He then left his little hell and back to earth he flew
Went straight into Westminster to put his ideas through
He touched them very all very lightly with his little fork
And made them spend the money reprocessing in T.H.O.R.P.

"Yes we must build Trident" everyone did loudly cry
Even though it could explode us, up into the sky
We have to kill our enemy though they seem to be
Fathers, mothers, sisters, brothers, just like you and me.
Trident then was built
And the world was over spilt
With destructive weaponry
Hidden deep within the sea
Full of rotting radiation
Causing seeping devastation
And in depots underground, buried in extensive mound
Tended and defended with posts and wire around,
Stacked ready and waiting for the devil's deadly game.
He returned quite satisfied to the place from whence he came
And was almost happy from events he was expecting
Jumping high with joy to learn that man continued 'testing
He pulled the globe towards him and slowly turned it round
In many lands across the world he very easily found
BLOODSHED, WAR, DISASTER, man destroying man
And nuclear threat developing all the world to span

ALL FOR POWER FOR PROFIT, CAUSING PEOPLE STRIFE
STEALING WEALTH AND LABOUR AND ALSO TAKING LIFE.

ALL FOR POWER FOR PROFIT, MAKING WAR; TO SELL
SPOILING THE HEAVEN WE LIVE IN, CREATING LIVING HELL.

NATIONALISM

A battle fierce between each state
Each nation taught each state, to hate
Check points, barriers, to divide
People trained, ingrained, inside
Imagined line of difference
Under heavy sufferance
Of fabricated, fierce, conflict
Fearing an enemy who will inflict
An atrocious funeral pyre
Of bodies, building, bomb and fire
When wars despotic, mortal sin
Is made by ruling class within
In ruling calls itself the nation
Its people under domination
In the nations fragmentation
Rich and poor remain relation
When raping earths fine elements
Causes dire disfigurement
When fighting for earths rich resources
Compels aggression cruel and forces
Wars between each nation state
And manufactures nations hate

When all would be so simply spared
If all resources could be shared
To banish wealth and poverty
And end wars inhumanity

HOW DARE THEY..................?

1700-1900

How dared they, how dared they? raid Africa of men
Take strong built muscled beauty, confine within ships pen
Pack people head to toe with no space or air for breath
Below in darkness clamped in iron, to suffer choking death
In stench of human sickness from rolling of ships motion
Within a rocking tossing barge, a speck upon vast ocean
Sold as cheap commodity, to labour as a slave
From day to night, from youth to age, into a pauper's grave
Those who fled were hunted, persecuted to perdition
Spiked with metal round the neck, tortured to submission
Degraded, made to serve and coldly patronised
The beauty of a sun kissed skin, insultingly despised
Forced to sweating labour, in cotton fields white heat
Creating wealth for others, for them a cruel defeat.

How dared they, how dared they? force peasants off the land
Enclose the stolen soil with wall, turn them to hired hand
To labour as cheap wage slave in monstrous factory
Teeming millions packed in slums of pulsing poverty
Dragooned, berated, worked and worn, fed unwholesome fare
In prison to repeated action in fluff laden air
From shared bed, in cellar bred, with cobble, stone and brick
In smoke, in steam, a blackened stream, by coal and coke made thick
Hooting horn to drag from sleep, clacking clogs on ground
For hourly, daily, tending to clanging machine sound
In churches parsons promise a better life to follow
In pubs the alcohol will sop feeling of deep sorrow
Forced to sweating labour in mines dark blackened night
Chimneys belching blackening soot, blighting golden light.

How dared they, how dared they? oppress with fear and god
The weighty might all powerful to dominate roughshod
Heavy churches in cramped streets in village, city, town
Subservient people on their knees, eyes closed, head bowed down
Harangued from upraised pulpit to conform to power
Of those who use omnipotence to steal each working hour
From those who have ingested inferiority
From those of overpowering superiority
Humbling words of guilt and fault from the pulpit fell

Landing in the minds below promise of fierce hell
For those who dared to disobey the orders of religion
Unholy fire or holy love, concocted, sanctioned, vision
With pomp, with arts, with worship, is raised the tower of Babel
With gods, the myth for dominance, a great imagined fable.

How dared they, how dared they? force people into sheds
Concentrate in wooden shacks with tiered bunks for beds
Confine them to a ghetto, weakened by starvation
To a heap of skeletons, a once proud healthy nation
Prisoners of hunger, eyes empty, heavy head
Stick arms, stick legs, weak shuffling and ragged mounds of dead
Crammed in trains dark airless trucks to chambers full of gas
Or shot to slither down the slopes of a deep morass
Discarded in a gulag with ignorant oppression
Disregarded, tortured with hideous aggression
Again are people conquered, again are utilised
Held as captive labour, again to be despised
Refugees through boundaries, masses ebb and flow
A moving sea of dereliction through mud ice and snow.

How dare they, how dare they? create destructive force
Remove fine natural elements, build vile weapons coarse
To blast whole cities from the earth in ominous explosion
And force the young to slaughter with national devotion
People of each nation run in panic helter-skelter
Into safe dark womb of earth, underground find shelter
As silently above, through clouds, released iniquity
On all those unaware below of gross ferocity
Melted, scorched and blasted to exist no more
Are a nation's innocents, destroyed by wasteful war
Great the wealth created from labour concentrated
Used for savageness in wars by rulers perpetrated
Desperate is the longing for their wars to cease
Desperate is the hoping for water, food and peace.

How dare they, how dare they? make learning a class tool
Keep children captive hourly imprisoned in a school
For wealth to buy the privilege of knowledge for the power
To rule divided nation of higher, middle, lower
To select, decide, make plain a clear divide
Impose a cruel injustice on those who are denied

Measuring with examination in a rigid game
Compelling competition or coercing to feel shame
Great goddess meanly given, has soaring wings impaired
Falls to ground, becomes unsound, if not justly shared
Cramped within, rendered thin, by wretched hierarchy
Harsh despair clouds round her fair and noble destiny
To comprehend the passing blend of nature, life and art
To civilize, to freely rise and ignorance depart.

How dare they, how dare they? make profit the main aim
Organize, control all life, for excessive gain
With money as the god and profit as a king
Compel worldwide production for their profiting
Fear of hunger, loss of pay, looming poverty
Persuasive propaganda and cold necessity
Drive each person to accept cheap sale from those who buy
Energy or learned skill of mind, of hand, of eye
With army, tank and gun, with baton of brute force
Gods and kings of money ride an oppressive course
To kill the just demand of those who would be free
From the domination of exploiting thievery
Money's force, despotic, shapes an ordained way
Burdens all with tyranny, crippling new born day.

How dare they, how dare they? send millions off to fight
In clash for wealth cruel empires cast on the world their blight
Force youth to learn to slaughter, to maim, to die, to kill
Until whole massacre exhausts embattled human will
To conquer with destruction using weapons to excess
For some to claim a victory supposed a success
In misery, in suffering, of fathers, mothers, sons
Sisters, daughters slaughtered and anguished little ones
Disrupted, made corrupted, by inculcated hate
The manufactured soldiery destroying other state
Shattered buildings, scattered limbs, spilt blood; explosions flame
The sacrifice of innocence, innocent of blame
For war not of their making, of benefit to none
Ruination of creation until the fight is done

How dare they, how dare they? spill rich young blood on street
Pierce bravery with bullets, assault, punch, kick and beat
To curb with force, turn back the course, of just revolution
'Gainst unarmed people, unafraid, imbued with resolution

Mangled leg, dangling arm, lolling head, limp hand
Supine the line of bloodied death, no more upright to stand
Rushed on rough cart, by loving hands, bloodstained cloth, shed tear
Above all heads, by loving arms, carried high on bier
All minds incensed, all-powerful, great rising inspiration
A tight packed mass, a moving stream, with strong determination
To change dictatorship of wealth, at whatever cost
To end crude state brutality, however life is lost
A many bodied action, truth as compelling guide
Creating for humanity, liberty worldwide.

Now dare we, now dare we, end class society
End wealth empowered to cruel rule, imposing poverty
Causing wars destruction goading every soul
Concentrating labour to a soul destroying goal
For some to be in palaces with high walls to protect
Others in a shanties filth, foul water to infect
No more will most be labouring, for others wealth to reap
No more will vicious weaponry in subjugation keep
No riches will be owned by one, extracted from the other
Every person valued, precious to one another
And justice, breadth of knowledge will feed a common will
And feelings great will arts inspire to cause our hearts to fill
No more to be exploited destroyed and crucified
To rise in happiness and love for life now beautified.

The gods have died and with the gods, the kings
A shell remains as spirit spreads its wings
Belief has flown and empty is the mind
Of former thoughts, weak wreck is left behind
The rule of princes, gods and fantasy
Remain as ruined, crumbled fallacy
A wind sweeps on to banish monarchy
Wild whirlwinds blast from wealth its hierarchy
Powers that were, rage in futility
Opposing with a vile brutality
Forcing back with hopeless aim the form
Taking shape as nature builds a storm
And from on high, descends to cleanse the earth
As re-formation makes a fresh rebirth.

WAR AND REVOLUTION

War and revolution, revolution war
Capital rampages Earth tearing with its claw
Crushing opposition with weapons in full force
Oppressing for its profits people in its course

Fighting for world resources all life to buy and sell
Forcing the world populace to its form of hell
Clever minds and fingers of all humanity
Are caught consumed and channelled in conformity

It dominates the waking hours of world population
To manipulate their powers in its calculation
Activity is overlaid by its tight restraint
Ev'ry person ev'ry thing o'er shadowed by constraint

Exploiting others traps in bondage each society
Jailors stay incarcerated with captivity
Money's wars infect all minds with vile contamination
Causing bitter anguish by its brutal perpetration

Marching feet raised arm salute sceptre ball and crown
Gods dictators hierarchy keep each people down
Slave or peasant servant clerk or capital's wage labour
Paper money coin or card control human endeavour

Drilled into the factory to produce its goods
Saturate world markets with commodities in floods
Dominate with Empire fight Empire to demise
With war to fill the air with screaming anguished cries

Energy and youth is sapped from working populations
To produce vile weaponry and hurl at other nations
Diabolical the force for human life destruction
Of millions blinded wounded killed by wars bloodied construction

Buildings streets and cities razed unto the ground
Rubble rough wall broken splintered to a mound
Soft sweet flesh of babies crushed in cement dust
Buried smashed surrounded by sharp angled crust

Metal shells exploding pouring fierce flamed fire
Bursting black clouds breaking growing ever higher
Hollow window spaces non-existent doors
Tilted piled obscenely are shattered lurching floors

Many poor but more and more money spent to kill
Threatening all people with atomic overspill
Pressure on one button with one finger's silent stealth
Causes instant death below to retain the wealth

Polluting mighty oceans with a deadly freight
Poisoning unfortunates within a moneyed fate
None escape beyond all trapped within the heap
Many scrabbling for an existence low and cheap

Distress Fear and Anger from Nuclear Weaponry
Dismay sickened misery from vast polluted sea
Teeming coloured coral empty still white dead
Stomach filled with plastic by caring parents fed

Accumulated residue in monstrous deadly mound
No place found to store it no place underground
Pile on poisonous pile persisting centuries
For the children yet unborn a bequeathed dis-ease

Cruel the schools of organized inferiority
Unjust the false creation of superiority
Difference of manner dividing snobbery
From conscious capital's unfair and blatant robbery

Past religions fail the aim to contain to bind
Replaced by new technology to control the mind
Rulers harsh continue with murderous suppression
Now a biased media can aid a cruel oppression

Art corrupted fiercely to a fractured waste
Capital's distortion degrades artistic taste
Its false creations empty or tortured forms uncouth
Replace subjective vision of objective truth

Within unjust society is art caught in a mould
A rarefied commodity to be bought and sold

Expressive of lost content vacuous weak contorted
Discordant sick deranged by falsity distorted

Convulsed by a severe disease is art's modernity
Divorced extracted stolen from our broad community
Fine works of past creation stand as great achievement
Art now from noble inspiration suffers a bereavement

Taxes rates insurance bills burden every wage
Shelter houses flats and shops are charged at every stage
Food and water light and heat basic need is met
Laden with profit grasping at the highest price firm set

Rent and mortgage credit debt higher purchase hock
As the hard god profit cheats our anxious flock
Constant worship with desire infects our human will
As burdening necessity directs our human skill

Plentiful fertility though many suffer need
Surfeit unrelated creates a wealthy greed
Nature's rich abundance is distortingly impaired
As money's imposition cripples life unfairly shared

Crippled nations industry from markets over showered
Crippled labour's misery from wages underpowered
Without work forced to shirk from rewarding rise
Unemployed life unenjoyed fed ignoble lies

Gambling on the stock exchange for rich dividends
Following percentages of profits latest trends
From intensive labour of long hours of deprivation
In sweatshops for the excess wealth from human degradation

Accumulated money in exclusive concentration
Amassed the stolen riches in lavish saturation
Spent on deep indulgence or cautious re-investment
Or lofty towers or armaments for future re-enrichment

Guilt filled charity is given to appease the heart
To release the conscience from a sharp and pain filled dart
From knowledge of the suffering of poor majority
With knowledge of the benefits from tax free charity

For those are worshipped for the wealth which they did not create
And hide in high walled palaces behind protective gate
For from the milling millions who die in cheap disposal
Is extracted excess as they're under wealth's imposal

Within unequal social form grows conscious opposition
Which ripens to rejection of despotic imposition
For few with most and most with less has to be addressed
For the great majority are by the few oppressed

Capital's development produces rich abundance
Showering the favoured few with empty opulence
Competition strives to win wealth's supremacy
Of one against another to cause discrepancy

Buying cheap and selling dear reigns as every rule
In office shop or showroom college house and school
Forcing those in competition to achieve its aim
An energetic push for profit reaping golden gain

The banks decline and fall reveals crisis capital
Suspicion fear surveillance is a measure of its pall
Its cruel wars of empire its army its police
Cannot restrain the power of wage slavery's release

Release for most develops fast until the rulers fall
Justice rises to take place in cities streets for all
Change of power to the ruled a new condition flows
Within most minds the opening flower of revolution grows

Revolt now battles strongly to defeat unhappiness
Against authoritarian crime rise actions to redress
Injustice murder suffering a cruel persecution
Toward the innocent and those in rising revolution

Soldiers guns soldiers crimes cannot defeat the brave
Who learn through human suffering to ignore the grave
So called governments corrupt with force of their repression
Battle hard though lose to continue harsh aggression

Now grows the task which history asks when justice starts its reign
Now breaks the hour when change in power frees all to life re-gain
And tyranny defeated by classless society
Allows with noble purpose a shared prosperity

For each to live an enriched life in precious Liberty
For none to reap an excess wealth from pain-filled poverty
Equality creates the trust for great Fraternity
When wage slaves free themselves worldwide and raise humanity

Nature's grand magnificence be honoured with due care
Its richness power and beauty no longer to impair
Our minds iron bound by money from its confine gain release
To expanding heights uplifting creative life increase

------------0------------

Postscript

No need now for rich or poor
We do not want your weaponry we will not have your war
Nature's rich abundance turns US to rich from poor
No need for hunger, poverty or misery from crime
The world is full of beauty, wealth abundantly divine
Our purpose we'll fulfil and each a life refine
Joy and friendship shared, the love for ALL sublime.

BUILDINGS, PEOPLE AND CHANGE

Prologue

Slashed by rain, wild wind, harsh sun
Or conflicting, fighting man
Showing through sharp, splintering sand
Are past constructions, a wasteland
Mound on mound, buried deep
In measureless, eternal sleep
Fragments, ruins, a shattered crust
Their scattered elemental dust
Far flung, by winds dispersing gust
Reconstructed by fresh hand
Across deep seas, projecting land
On which in turn, they firmly stand
Then in time, engulfed they lie
Return to earth, dissolve and die

Imperative necessity
Makes idea reality
Ethereal imagination
Creates material formation
Innumerable possibility
Simplicity to complexity
Creation, new development
For benefit, excitement
Discovery, appreciation
Of natures varied compilation
Change within the human mind
Uplifting, moulding, humankind
Great the joy we have on earth
Creating, making and rebirth

BUILDINGS, PEOPLE AND CHANGE

Cathedrals, castles, churches, down
Relics of Feus' mighty crown
Castles now a craggy rubble
Mounds of rugged lumps with stubble
Irregular, with plants to cover
Black plumed birds who cruise and hover
Broad were walls, stone, heavy, strong
Helmeted, the conquering throng
Sword fights on high spiral stair
Imposing bold will everywhere
Doling stolen land in parcels
Warring, defending, wealth in castles
Vanished, gone, their mighty thrones
Their power, crumbled to mere stones

Cathedrals stand inspired membrane
And rise, their soaring heights attain
Expressions of minds lofty aim
To wealth, to beauty, from earth born
From backs of labouring peasants torn
Their aspiring splendour made
With murder in a far Crusade
With ritual, prayers and reprimands
With downcast eyes and upturned hands
Reverence for pervasive God
Extracting wealth from sheep and sod
Forcing peasants to pay them tithes
Religion permeating lives
Their piety, power, a doomed demise

Cathedrals changed, for mind has flown
Toward commerce power has grown
Bishop turned from cleric to "boss
And profits filled the spirits loss
Shops with goods, throbbing with shoppers
Pouring wealth into vast coffers
Goods and money, money, goods
Flowing through like veins of blood
Keeping counting houses high
Boxes scraping clouds and sky

These, the new cathedrals stand
Round each city, in each land
Monster oblongs of blank glass
Squares of dullness, crude and crass

Cement grey tenements nearby
On balconies, bikes, washing dry
For wage slaves of each differing nation
For housing, for their exploitation
In office, shop or factory
Forced there by necessity s
Motorways for mile on mile
Monuments to 'modern' style
Hotels, luxury to pamper
Seller, buyer or consumer
Alcohol, in bar, taverna
The emptiness within to smother
Crime, corruption, to possess
Wealth created by the mass

Splendid rooms with gilded doors
Sculpted ceilings, spacious floors
Noble, balanced, the structure stands
On labouring slaves in far off lands
Aristocrats who did not toil
Rich, superior, owned the soil
Servants, servicing their need
Their demands, their grasping greed
On wealth resulting from the trade
Plentiful, the mansions made
Stone constructed in fine piles
Woodlands stretching round for miles
All vacated, now for visitors
Paying to view them as spectators

The grand town house is up for rent
Front garden filled with grey cement
Cars at many angles placed
The pompous frontage now defaced
Inside, divided, large rooms are
To bedrooms, bathrooms, kitchens, bar
Flats for new young customers
Which once contained stiff housekeepers

Maidservants carrying coals or tea
The 'madam' ordering bossily
Rooms furnished full to overflowing
Gas lamps after sundown glowing
Plush lawned gardens sold and built on
A mode of living now a bygone

Dominant, the chimney high
Rising up to grey cloud sky
Black, the choking smearing smoke
Huge, the factory's stone block
Crammed, the crashing machinery
Long, the hours of drudgery
For hundreds, thousands of hands and hearts
Tending, demanding metal parts
The cotton stretching, pulling tight
Darkened by fluff, the cloudy light
Now changed, divided to small compartments
New kitchens, bedrooms, tiny apartments
For single persons, living alone
All the frantic activity gone

Across the countryside are farms
The house surrounded by new barns
Sheds for milking saddened cows
Cramped, confined are fattening sows
Chickens turned to battery hens
Bath in metal prisons penned
Corrugated iron on steel
For lightless calves turned into veal
Confining animals for slaughter
Exported, crushed in caged transporter
Exchanged as a commodity
By economic authority
For us to eat as cannibals
The tortured flesh of animals

The old barns, some neglected, left
To crumble, empty, now bereft
Bought by a developer
Restructured the interior
Plastered walls, new ceilings, beams
Under flooring heat in seams

Sofas in new sitting rooms
Closets housing showers or brooms
Once filled with swollen uddered cows
Once hay or pigs or chickens housed
All changed, unrecognisable
Past sound and scent, unrepeatable
Gone the horse, the cart, the plough
So different, the then and now

Side by side in road or street
Stand houses, duplicate and neat
Pavements built with squares of stone
Smothering the Earth's rich loam
Hedges, driveways, gates, small lawn
Chimneys, windows, doors, to form
Row on row of nests of brick
Dashed with pebbles, covered thick
Perhaps two cars to stand outside
On the tarmacadamed drive
Dogs and children, both emerge
To run on pavements grass edged verge
And out in ever growing spread
Millions working for their bread

Stone church building now degraded
Passed purpose preaching, disregarded
Empty, sold, pulled down or changed
Original purpose now de-ranged
A new religion, commercialism
To the people constantly given
Through all media and television
In every dwelling, every nation
Permeating its negation
Calculated the imposition
Upholding, forcing, ruling vision
Old religions thinking, past
Decreasing, waning, sinking fast

The corner shop, a transformation
Suffering a consummation
Outside the town, new magnetism
A temple to consumerism

Through glass automatic door
Stacked with goods, extensive floor
And supermarkets parking space
A large and fleeting meeting place
Millions in a constant flow
To come, to fill, to buy, to go
Wheels on trolleys, cars on wheels
Both stacked up with peoples' meals
Fulfilling a new unstated law
That we continue to buy more

For many buildings, tragedy
Neglected, broken, wantonly
Their beauty, richness, artistry
Dispersed, wasted, carelessly
Instead remain small bungalows
Or bland dull housing in long rows
Skyscraper blocks with blank windows
The matchbox 'Bauhaus' influence
Deadly result of violence
Or 'modern' buildings convolution
Styled 'progressive' revolution
Now replaced in town's high street
Proud stone buildings with new concrete
Shabby, becoming obsolete

Central to city, tremendous power
Huge palace, dome, above all tower
Gilded throne, ceremonious seat
Carpets soft for "Your Grace's feet
Mirrors, lights, reflecting gold
Pomp, privilege, to uphold
Promoting capacious revenue
And adulatory retinue
"Your Excellence", "Right Honourable",
"Your Majesty", "Most Venerable",
"Serene High-ness" more sycophancy
For proud pedantic supremacy
Change is now for the body politic
Replacing Royalty with a Republic

Peasants green leafed cultivation
Smothered by cruel deprivation
Land, small home, stolen, enclosed
Destroyed, churned up, scraped, bulldozed
Forced to build in grey cement
Steel girdered, square, high tenement
Close packed cities, office blocks
Car choked roads, stocked with shops
All things to be bought and sold
Every mind concerned with gold
More yet more, shipped in supply
Plastic toys to pacify
A longing within us to deny
To return to earth and sky

In long sheds low, cheap, to compete
Heat, machinery, to maltreat
Girls and women, ever sewing
Created items ever growing
In sweatshops, profits organiser
Subjecting them to supervisor
And unjust inequality
Of hardened profitability
Living confined in poverty
Labouring long from necessity
For a minute part of the equity
Though this arrangement need not be
An end will come to its misery
Abolishing world wage slavery

War, war, war seems evermore
Buildings shot, no roof, no floor
Crumbling walls, thin shell expose
Gaps, with sharpened smashed windows
Jagged, mangled, tangled crust
Broken, shattered, matted dust
Cities, towns: flattened, erased
People burnt, destroyed and crazed
In dampened, darkened cellar hiding
Scarce protection for surviving

To escape iniquity
Sent through air or land or sea
From those contemptuous of life
Who manufacture conflict, strife

Resistance grows, the mind contains
Energy, hope and strong high aims
Through war and suffering it remains
Movements huge as waves on sea
Uplift, peak, swell humanity
Ebb and flow as waves on shore
Rolling back to meet one more
Opposing wind, cold soaking rain
Through jungle, city, rough terrain
With suffering, war and intense pain
Mind retains the supposition
That necessary is opposition
Culminating, vast the range
Eternal permanence of change

Epilogue

From world mass the people give
Labour, wealth, for some to live
In mansion or in palace large
When they in slum and shanty starve

Toiling precious hours away
For life deprived and on 'low pay
Little money and propaganda
Force the body and mind to labour

To slave, to stave off anxiety
Caused by hunger's extremity
To pay a mortgage or large bill
Support the young, their stomachs fill

Governments the wealth control
Business big has large payroll
In exchange for time and labour
Pay low wages for the favour
Profits creamed as froth on beer
Buying cheap and selling dear
Defending wealth by making war
Attacking other nations poor

But all things change, are refutable
No thing remains immutable
As shown by buildings of the past
Power structures do not last

Again is time for wealth to change
From gambling rule of stock exchange
Owned and played by business' class
Creating, forcing a labouring mass

Into imposed wage slavery
Unjust, class based society
Concomitant brutality
Destruction, criminality

The time has come for wealth to pass
To working mass, to end all class
Changing for all humanity
Wealth, war, hunger, poverty

For us to share fraternity
To care with magnanimity
To live with equanimity
In liberty, equality

-----000-----

Gifted to us from the past
A legacy which long will last
From ancients in cruel slavery
Their work, uprising, bravery

Though vicious punishment was meted
Their hopes, their actions, undefeated
Changing for all a social structure
Producing new a counterculture

Throughout our lives, their lives remain
Their thoughts and actions we contain
In our mouths the sounds we use
Past generations have infused

Letter on tablet, a little shape
Together a boundless world remake
In our extensive libraries
Shelves of past discoveries
Our minds exalted by their stories
Of hopes, of gains, of loss, of glories

Uplifted by heart's sweet emotion
Images from art's devotion
Reflecting through the hand and mind
All aspects of our humankind
Sculptured image from hard stone
That lies beneath our enriched loam

Rich the cultivated soil
Developed by incessant toil
Covering, our food to yield
The world with furrowed, fertile field

Music, to the minds delight
Inspired, illuminating height
Athletics, dance, a deep enchantment
Beauty, grace in body's movement

Physicians, knowledge, tested skill
Study of the systems ill
Striving to remove disease
Suffering to try to ease

Math'matics measured calculation
Deducing, numbered clear relation
Engineers of iron and water
Arched aqueducts diverting river
From all beings of the past
Contribution to us, vast
As nothing does the same continue
And dying form will life renew
We in turn do give and pass on
A legacy: re-generation

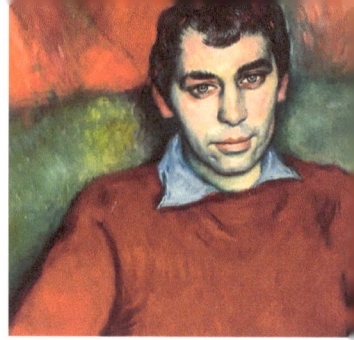

RACE

Nature's cornucopia abundantly is spilled
Everywhere around us, our minds are richly filled
And wonder at variety, unlimited and fine
All forms large and small, possess unique design
Is there any living being among this copious land
That you leave undisturbed with your destructive hand
Most of all your fellow man, is it not the greatest sin
To hurt and kill because there is a difference of a skin.

MONEY

When we were young and growing strong, lack of money ground you
down
Removed the smile from your fine face, replaced it with a frown.
Your life was contained by worry, money was in short supply
Many times a look of despair would darken your clear blue eye
Then tears would fill and overspill and I would wish to die.

Money, cruel fabrication of mankind, a tyrant whose filthy stain
Permeates our lives, crucifies our minds, is created and forged in pain
It strides giant steps across the surface of the world,
life cannot exist without its blight
Hunger trembles slowly, weakly moves its heavy head
and tens of millions suffer the cruel plight
Youth's high hopes fall to despair, lie numbed upon the ground
Women are bought and sold for its sake and love is debauched for a
pound
Poverty corrodes the life and throws the spirits into hell
Wealth corrupts and to extend its realm all life and soul will sell.

Money dictates the peace or strife
Money decides on death or life
Money feeds or makes hunger grow
Money causes the blood to flow.

Money, I hate you truly for your inequality
For the myths you perpetuate of superiority
All the waste and suffering caused indiscriminately
I loathe your very existence and would kill your pernicious spell
Gather up your scattered coins and cast them into hell.

NO MONEY

"Add another nought, dear
Or maybe two or three
To the cheque that you are writing
Then pass it on to me

Its so easy for you to draw
A little circle to give me more
A little world like a sun to me
Makes happiness from misery

For nought means nothing
And from nothing comes
But by adding many noughts
Can produce enormous sums

You see, from nought
Which can be taught
And shown it to be right
That by adding many noughts
Becomes its opposite!"

HIGH PRICE ADVICE

"Buy it cheap and sell it very dear, dear
You will make a profit never fear, dear
That's the thing that you should try to do, dear
Then buy "stocks and shares' as we all do, dear

You'll change from being poor to being rich, dear
Leave others to be cold and in the ditch, dear
Why should you care, how others fare and what they do, dear
Buy it cheap and sell it dear, will see you through, dear

Then you can buy the newest shiny car, dear
Have drinks, expensive dinners in the bar, dear
Wear the smartest fashions in your clothes, dear
Bleach your hair, enlarge your bust and change your nose, dear

To gain the richest spouse that you can bind, dear
To buy the richest house that you can find, dear
And go for lounging holidays abroad, dear
And never mind if you are feeling bored, dear

You'll see the 'high-ups' making guns to sell, dear
Causing others pain and perfect hell, dear
It's clear they will engulf us in their wars, dear
Don't bang your head so hard against their walls, dear

You can wreck yourself on deadly drugs and drink, dear
No need to rack your brains to try to think, dear
If your heavy heart is sad and sick with sorrow, dear
You can always kill yourself upon the morrow, dear"

DOUBLOONS

Money must go, money must now be-gone
Its racking burden lifted from each one
Once golden piece, piled high like shining moon
Dream of people to light their deepest gloom
Coins with sovereign head to pass to hand
Exchanging all in each wealth driven land
To buy, to sell, to cheat, to gain, to kill
With energy, worldwide, with ruling will
To keep in chains of poverty, the mass
To laden with abundance golden ass
Weighted with wealth, torn from nature's aeons
From rock, with skill and sweat of millions
Its tricks, its theft, its debt, profit and loss
Go from the mind, go from our hopes, as dross.

Bountiful is bursting reproduction
Powerful its aim of reconstruction
Plentiful rich seed by nature given
Forest lush, seas teeming, create heaven
Seed from one tree could make woodlands flourish
Laden fruit from one could many nourish
Corn with fattened multi-seeded head
Could fill all aching emptiness with bread
De-salinated sea could channelled flow
Moisten dry desert, fertile soil to grow
Money imposed with harsh deprivation
To necessity adds complication
Unequal wealth unlicensed does restrain
As many strive to thrive in life in vain

The beauty of all lands its drive destroys
Flays animals, traps men and blights their joys
Its lack produces swollen hunger's pain
Its excess, monster piles of selfish gain
Its snobbery and inequality
It prostitutes our pure fertility
Craftiness and wily-eyed extortion
Twisting honesty to a distortion
Wealth's bitter wars conflicting cruelty
Soaked full of bloodied criminality
All nature to be bought and all things sold
Reducing aims to grovelling for gold
Without pernicious wealth we could be free
To live, to love, to grow in harmony.

WHAT FOUL OBSCENITY IS THIS?

What foul obscenity is this?
Soft flesh we worship with a kiss
Pierced by metal, flowing, bleeding
Red the oozing matter seeping
Destructions devilish intent
From high majestic sky is sent
Lozenge metal, heavy, monstrous
Unleashed, striking the unconscious
To aim to cause the greatest harm
To tear through torso, leg and arm
To rip fine cheek, fine lip, fine eye
Be blown dispersed, fragmented die
Who doth use and misuse our times?
To perpetrate their blood-filled crimes

What foul obscenity is this ?
Sweet flesh we honour with a kiss
Sick stick like babies rendered small
For want of sustenance for all
Lie many far too gaunt to cry
Or suckle empty breast nearby
When drought with hunger cloud their life
Reduced by internecine strife
Of persecution bomb and gun
For Mother, baby, daughter, son
All shelter strafed, to live in fear
All hope, all life, all those held dear
Destroyed, to lie in heaps of rubble
In pain, distress, despair, trouble

What foul obscenity is this ?
For flesh adored by a kiss
Nature rich, with plenty given
Gives us worldly dream of heaven
Where beauty reigns and all are free

From all retarding poverty
From false wealth's degrading power
Kills to build an empty tower
From hard conforming tyranny
Of hour, of day, wage slavery
Ruled not by gods, but flesh built man
Who turn the great to lowly span
Turn happiness to misery
Obscenity which need not be

J'Accuse

They are hungry and could be fed
You send them bullets made of lead
They are poor and clothed in rag
You send to them a body bag
Their shelter from the heat of sun
You destroy with drone and bomb
They would rest in peace and sleep
Soldiers cruel cause them to weep
Dark seeds of hatred and dissent
You spread with weeds of discontent
And with your soldiers ugly boot
Imprison, torture, random shoot
And for your Empire in decline
You fill wide world with vicious crime

Your tower is built on shifting sand
From other's labour, mind and hand
Obscenity cannot prevail
Fear departs, leaves not a trail
Golden coins which earth disgorged
Will change by the same hand that forged
The mass cannot be ruled by few
With cruelty and words untrue
For they will force and they will break
Thick fetters which injustice make
Your order, rule, disorder brings
And wealth for tyrants, despots, kings
Your theft, with wars obscenity

Will end with true equality.
Each one and all, each birth the same
By one route to earth we came
Swollen with life, creative womb
Brings forth new being from the tomb
Growth, which permeates all things
Unfolds, develops, upward brings
Enlightenment, uplifting strives
Towards illuminating lives
Where man-made suffering may cease
Give wealth in happiness and peace
All given, shared, nurturing care
To grow in stature, beauty fair
Strong, kind, just, the mind inspiring
With truth, with trust, nobly aspiring

PALESTINE

Brutality unyielding
Swaggering soldiers wielding
Mothers, fathers, shielding
Soldiers occupying
Suicides defying
Bravely face expiring
Helicopters firing
Bulldozers despoiling
Peoples life destroying
Tanks rolling and gunning
Little children running
Women weeping, crying
Little children dying.

"A refugee in your own land
A refugee in stone and sand
Although you live in Palestine
This land is ours, your house is mine
We won it all in six day war
Defeated, now you can be sure
Your life, your land, we now possess
We occupy, suppress, oppress
Jerusalem, our Holy City
The wall we kiss, no human pity
Our soldiers show when they hunt down
Resistance fighters in your town
We have buried you alive
Your breath and body we divide
Our drones have targeted and spied
There is no place for you to hide
With bombs and bullets you are driven
In hundreds you are in our prison
Your sweet child is not exempt
From our murderous punishment
If they throw stones, we will not spare
If they die, or wounded are
We will shoot, we do not care
From the sea our rockets hurl
On sandy beach, the little girl

Is all that's left, her family
We blew into eternity.
Although in thousands you have died
Cheap labour, for us, you provide
You are poor but we're supported
By dollars, stealthily imported
Which pay for weapons for the wars
We perpetrate for dollars cause
We don't accept your Hamas vote
And we'll apply an antidote
And cut the money for your bread
And care not if you all lie dead
Dividing wall you cannot venture
Beyond its line you must not enter
With our check points, we control
Every movement, though we stole
To build our houses on your land
Reducing you to stone and sand"

You Murder Little Children
To KISS the Dusty Wall
If you could LOVE all Children
Barriers might fall.

WEALTH AND POVERTY

From stolen land enclosed by walls
Deprived, the labouring peasant falls
To cram stone streets, dark factory
With teeming rag filled misery
From destitute humanity
Was wealth produced in quantity

From freedoms sun, their beauty brown
Their dignity by crime brought down
Sold, shackled, slashed with whips
Fettered in hold of festering ships
By torture forced to slave, to sweat
And from their labour, wealth beget

The Indian Brave for land was killed
The blood of his Bison freely spilled
Across from Europe, impoverished pour
The fight for soil causes murderous war
To build high city and fill huge town
With wealth for the rich and the poor ground down

As Empires spread their domination
Atrocious, cruel, the degradation
Sour, the dose the people given
By war and famine they were driven
By force, subdued and terrified
Attacked, invaded, occupied

Now a rising has o'er turned
Their rule, their force, is justly spurned
Empires lose on every hand
And have to forfeit stolen land
Shrink and shrivel, becoming naught
From strong resistance, bravely fought

In our minds a change is surging
Through the old shell, just emerging
For our world we must be caring
Its resources all are sharing
As Empires powers fail, diminish
Its wars against us all will finish

LIBERATION?

You're the enemy, you lying old swine"*
Your speeches covering heinous crime
Sitting above at Conference table
Misleading speeches to enable
Perpetrations of world distortion
Extracting, torturing, for extortion
Admission of an innocent's guilt
Beyond: millions, their red blood spilt
Gulags, murder camps, cold and hunger
Secret' police, spies, fear and danger
Mothers distraught, caught in slaughter
Losing husband, son and daughter
Celebrations' loud marching boots
With gun and uniform, giving salutes
Proudly showing obscene creation
Huge metal bomb to frighten a nation
Rolling with threats of death, destruction
Behind the speeches, the cruel action
And in the name of Liberation
And freedom from a dark oppression
A fierce and bestial insanity
Ever suffered by humanity

*A remark called from the floor of a conference.

ART REFLECTING DECAY

Here staggers Art, with wan sick looks
Trailing palette, music, books
Sockets empty, holes of hell
Dis-ease etching every cell
Her noble former self is dead
Worms devour, grow in her head
Consume inspiring vision there
Confusion, gutter filled despair
For what to say, which way to go
She cannot tell, she may not know
Too weak, no standard can she bear
No hope, for lost is skill and care
A muddled mess from her entrail
Soils, stains, tears fine wedding veil

Listen, hear her sickened sound
Atonal music lurches round
Unresolved cacophony
A shapeless lack of harmony
Rhythm, profound melody
Are lost in empty novelty
Aspiring, inspired symphony
Buried in monotony
Susceptible, the senses falter
As taken are we to the altar
Given music's' bread and wine
Misled, by priest to think it fine
Death knell of our noble spirit
Until in time we rise above it

Her so called sculpture, shows for all
Forms incomprehensible
In cold white box of gallery
A temple for the mercenary
Distorted forms or none at all
Can leave us with an empty wall
Or mindless mess, muddled concoction
Emerge from lack of clear conviction
Gone majestic forms of beauty
Power, strength, purposeful duty

To render in carved reality
Figures of noble dignity
Or chiselled skilful low relief
Animal, flower, fruit or leaf

Her artists, reprehensible
Her art, incomprehensible
For the public, dichotomy
For the artist, lobotomy
Indulgence for the egoist
Retreat, complete, for the realist
Death of inspired observation
Disregarded, re-creation
Rejection of the substantial
Expressed the inconsequential
The non- representational
Presenting arts decline and fall
From vigorous salubrity
To diseased depravity

Within glass case, they stand displayed
Splendour from Euphrates made
Coiled by fingers nubile skill
Purpose, feeling, directing will
Pots, their curving beauty stands
From other times, from other lands
From mountains pulped to rivers' clay
Scooped out, malleable, baked to stay
Carried, balanced, with grace on head
For food, water, ashes of dead
Purpose, moulding, perfecting shape
Delight, design, to decorate
Now a pot of clay, hand thrown
Self-conscious, lumpy, ugly-grown

Throughout times past in differing ages
Woven, printed, dyed, cloth ranges
In shape, colour, to beautify
Or warmth, the body to supply
In twisted homespun thread on spool
Nimble fingers spinning wool

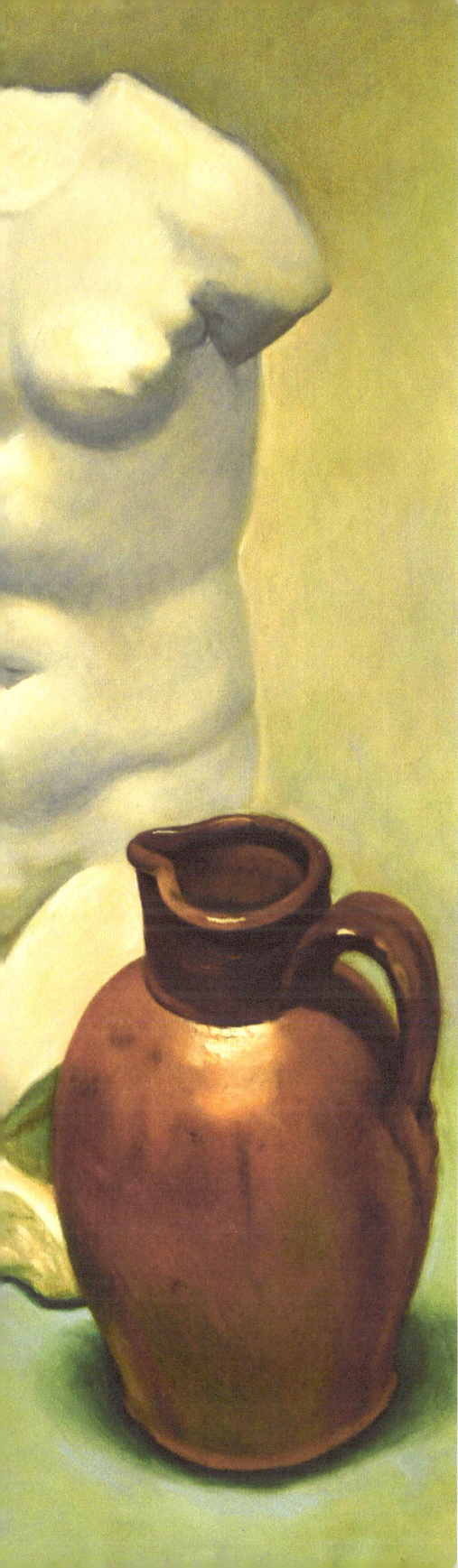

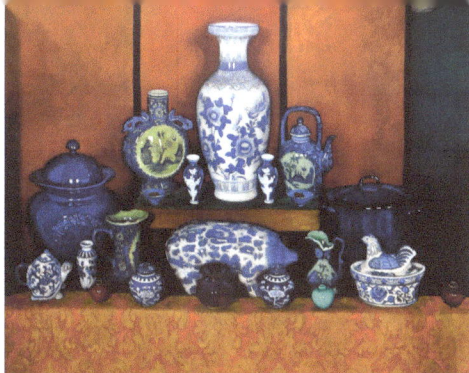

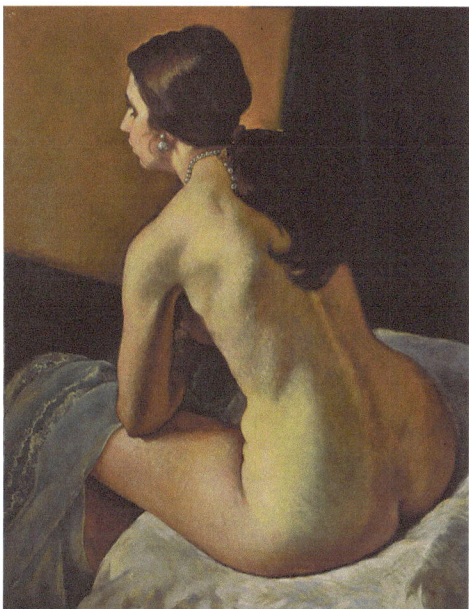

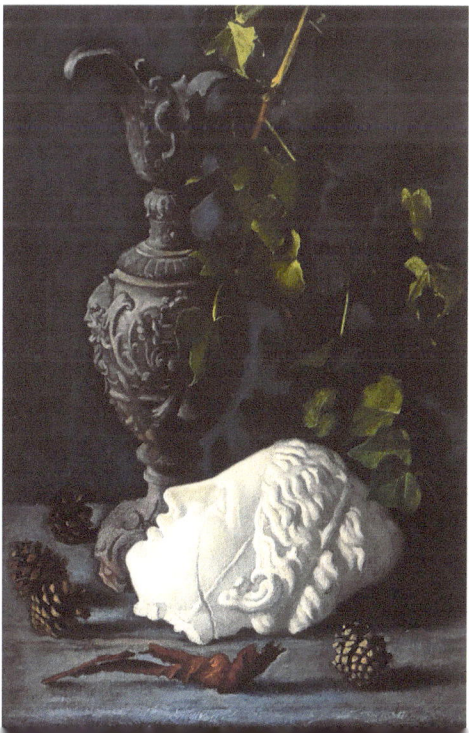

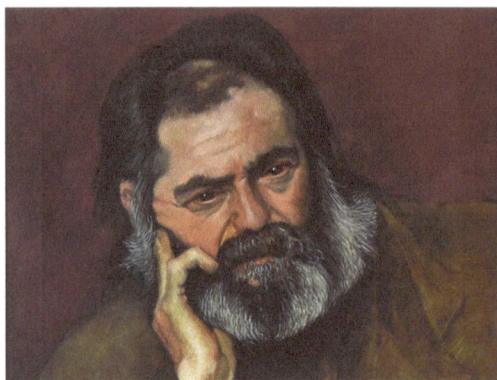

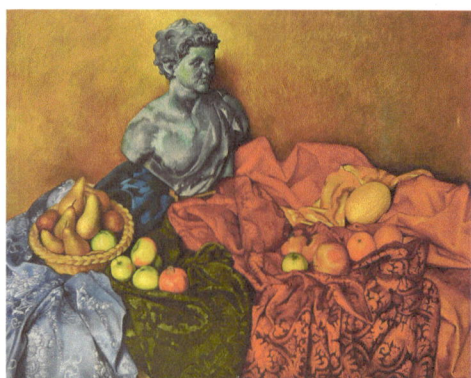

Or shining, silken, shimmering colours
Of silk from webbing caterpillars
In gorgeous dyes for graceful gown
From sandaled foot to draped head, crown
Or flowing robe or gathered tight
Smocked, embroidered, patterned bright
Now, in clothing of the West
Neurosis, dullness, is expressed

An endless list, the written word
A stew with pen, constantly stirred
By many hands readily lifted
By many minds readily sifted
Newspapers, books, magazines
Poured steaming daily from machines
To be devoured, read by millions
Informing, spreading ideas to billions
A thing we cannot live without
Bread and butter of hope or doubt
Arts decay spreads through the nation
Its wording feeding minds deflation
Despair, sadness, within creation
Until new thought brings great elation

See this small form carried round
A new born infant has been found
A Moses in the bulrushes
Or fire rekindled from cool ashes
Surviving, rescued, to arise
Grow, stand firm, uplifted eyes
Show mind of dreams and hopes, well filled
A hand, an arm, a body skilled
Well formed, well founded to rebuild
Preserve from hell, from wars' damnation
The world, the people of each nation
Fuse together a new relation
To turn from sadness, dire distress
To Arts' creative happiness

ANNE

Anne Dead ? Anne Dead ? No way ! No way !"
"Oh, yes, she died last Saturday"
It can't be so, it cannot be
All gone, her personality?
So full of life and sympathy
Anne, no, Anne cannot be dead
It turns all reason on its head
Her eyes so full of interest
Searching, roaming, come to rest
Make contact and a smile so kind
Showing generous lively mind
Her love for people old or young
For flowers on bushes in the sun
The children happy in her care
Time she gave, to all she'd share
Talk of how she'd grow her hair
Or how she's covering a chair
And "How is Ben, what is he doing
The wind her curls and blouse full blowing
Now she has gone, no more to be
Her presence never more we'll see
In shops where we would find her talking
Or pavements on which she'd be walking
Both emptied of her living being
Her life closed down, her eyes unseeing
Now she has gone and gone forever
And gone her life's full, rich endeavour
Of which remains in memory
A ghost of that which used to be.

Short the time since we did see
Her talking, laughing, recently
And thought she'd moved to warmer clime
With her new lover share her time
Though new relationship was made
With Death, involving soil and grave
Unwittingly against her will
The ground her bed, small part to fill

All movement gone, still, cold, she's laid
Warm lover's wishes, Death betrayed
Complete, a change, another being
Uncomprehending and unseeing
Permanent and everlasting
No air, no light, forever fasting
What is this Death? which quickly takes
And into other being makes
A lively mind, vital delight
And pitches it to darkest night
And turned by fire to ash and dust
To float on water or earth' s crust
Caressed by microbes, matter change
Their living purpose to arrange
Rebuild, remake, create new form
Enrich, for life to be reborn.

YOUNG MAN – A TRIBUTE

Doleful complaint is never uttered through his lips
Though malignancy invaded virile youth
Disease developed spreading wide its grip
Destroying his young manhood with uncouth
Corrupting power devouring every cell
So carefully built up in childhood growth
Turning to sickness, health, a living hell
Though he with jocularity fights through its spell

How deeply smothered can be youthful tear
Youthful suffering lies often buried deep
Allowing others not to see or hear
Heartache, masked or in dark hiding keep
Grown over with a cynic's layered despair
Healed wound concealing cruel calamity
No false bravado shown, the secrecy
Disguising pain internal with contumacy

Happy that from his loins, by-passed disease
Is born a healthy infant, wholesome, strong
With rosy growth developing to please
Though recent his own childhood, hardly gone
Early to fatherhood, paternity
Outwitting imperious death to now live on
Mocking, facing the probability
Of declining energy, finality.

ALCOHOLIC

Poor Chris, poor Christ, poor Christopher, lay dead upon the floor
No one found him, he lay there for three days or more

Everybody knew him as he shuffled round the town
His clothes and hair dishevelled, his face a puckered frown

A glint of recognition would sometimes light his eye
But soon it clouded over and in darkness he'd pass by

A photograph of him when young showed handsome smiling face
Besuited at a wedding before he lost the race

They said "He had a heart of gold, he was a gentle man"
Exposed to weather's heat and cold, drink shortened his life's span

Pretty rounded legs with shoes would smartly patter by
Oblivious in the doorway, the heap of Chris would lie

The steps of the memorial cross supported bright sweet flowers
Kindly words expressed the loss from those who shared his hours

"To Chris, gone to a better place" reflects sadness profound
For senses dimmed, the vivid world in alcohol is drowned.

HIGHLAND DANCER

She walked across with toe placed first upon the green grassed ground
Her hair was neatly, smoothly shaped and round her head was wound
A purple jerkin tight she wore which did full breast encircle
And on one foot she balanced, a perfect vertical

One arm a crook upon her side, to rest against small waist
The other lifted in a curve, above, and then replaced
Her kilt swung up and out and wide from vigour of her dance
Above each pretty pointing toe, she did all hearts entrance

We stand with feet upon the ground
Above our heads clear space
Our bodies firm to earth are bound
Our minds to boundless grace

We live a life unreasonable, with reason
Try to seize the unseizable, to give relief on
The senses, life is strange to us, is unpredictable
Eventful, favourable, unknowable
It grows and fluctuates, is uncontainable
Yet we contain it all, within our skull.

BIRTH OF A BABY

Perfection lies within my arm
Miniature of full grown man

Sweet, sweet, fineness, rosy cheek
Tiny lashes, nails and feet.

Oh, how strong the ecstasy
When first I heard and then saw thee

Nature's purpose ran through me
Her strong laws fulfilléd be

O'erpow'ring love swept over me
Before your birth I did not see

Life's force which so abundantly
Flows through every flow'r and tree

Nature's beauteous world is thine
And thou one part of her design

How I love thee, I adore
From your small form do I love more

Through you to all humanity
Embracing everyone I see

I can feel a power divine
A binding love, to us combine

From now on my heart's unfree
Ever more is bound to thee

Bondage welcome when I see
Your sweet form, so dear to me

Greater love there cannot be
Than the love, I feel, for thee.

A LAMENT – MOTHER

Where did you go ? I miss you so
I did not know - I loved you so

The blanket that you loved so much lies folded on the chair
If it could only cover you - if you were only there
With all the hopes you had for us, your dedicated care
All gone and with your precious dust, is vanished into air.

Your watch lies still and no more will your fingers ever wind
Your necklace you will never lift around your throat to bind
Against your pulse on neck and wrist firm circles they had made
Now an enfeebled loop describes within their coffin laid
Your home has changed, your treasures gone, your stick stands still beside
The empty table, flattened bed on which your body died.

DESPAIR OF DEATH

Knowing And Feeling

Why do we feel that birth is joy and death a tragedy
And have to live each day of life knowing our destiny?
Although in truth we little feel our own mortality
Most hours spent with rich intent, from thoughts of death, are free

Bud, flower, fruit and then the seed in warmth and light arise
Each progression in succession, quickly lives and dies
Swarms of men who walk today tomorrow will lie prone
Their labour done, their passion gone, their purpose yet unknown

The beech tree throws a million seeds to reproduce its life
So it seems, all living beings are to survive
Why do we live to think and feel, why should we be aware
And know that we must go from all we love and care?

When feeling the exquisite joy of being in the world
Knowing that our light will cease and darkness be unfurled
We live to be sure of nothing, save one clear certainty
The knowledge that our eyes will close and we will cease to be

MOTHER

Who swollen with new life, gave birth
Who nurtured, fed, clothed and soothed
Who comforted, removed our fears
Who smiled and wiped away our tears
Who hoped, who helped, who strived, who laboured
From minute, to hour, to month, to years
Unseen, unsung, unglorified

For Love

Your life is past
But you passed life on
And the love that you gave is alive
Is spread about among us all
And carried round inside
As part of a much greater love
We comprehend around
Though you have gone great love lives on

A Universal Sound

REGRET OF A SELFISH DAUGHTER

How wish and long to see
You return here to be
With us

Why did I not appreciate
To the full when you were here
And now a simple memory
Is something, treasured, savoured, dear
I long for you and wish and miss
Your presence here on earth
Life is sad and empty
Here, now, since your death

Your care I took for granted
Your constant interest
Devotion, dedication
Were of the finest
Your hopes for our wellbeing
Never wavered once
But I went through not heeding
And carelessly would dance across your feeling

Constant generosity
Of love and time you gave
And heedlessly took them
As my right to have
The greatest thing on earth
Unselfish mother love.

DEATH & REBIRTH

Grown old are we with withered countenance
Does clear reveal Time's lined provenance
As fragile veine^d leaf, lies fine, a skeleton
Delicate its tracery, roughly trod upon
Into the Earth enriching with remains
So we, lowered Earthwards, do enrich the same

Returning as dust to Earth from which we sprang
Great World, Great Mother, A round nurturing womb
Flesh building flesh from noble ecstasy
Developing in darkness, ripened, to break free
And burst to light, to air, to land, to sea
Part of World's particles, full life and Energy

FAITH

When lying on your dying bed
You smiled, "you must have faith" you said

Yes, dear mother, here's my faith, I know it will come to be
That those who labour will create, classless society
Though men are holding back the birth with utmost violence
With weapons which destroy the earth for power, for pounds, for pence

Capital's power is shattered, money has lost the crown
Deep cracks are in its edifice, its walls are tumbling down
Nothing is permanent, fixed or set, all will be replaced
By a new form, within the old one, now encased

Now the time is being born when class and race will cease
Divisions between us all will everywhere decrease
And rich and poor will disappear and we will live in peace
The womb is ripe and ready now, the labour of birth has begun
For us to live as we could live and value everyone
And love and care for all living beings who dwell beneath the sun.

MYTH, ART AND LOVE

Ye gods, hobgoblins, fairies, ye ghouls and devils small
Saints and "virgin" mothers are conjured up for all
By popes, by priests, by clergy, with holy-days and fasting
Fear of suffering, fire in hell with torment everlasting
Or float in clouds of blue and white with God high in the sky
Reward for burdened, laboured-life, given when you die
Non-sense lives and non-sense gives to life a vicious twist
Or adds a mad euphoria from things which don't exist
Fabricated freely from a world of myth and stone
Unreality conducts vast wealth up to its throne
From the tiny cranium of animal called Man
Intangible inventions rise, the whole world to span
From the Earth's resources are noble buildings fashioned
Soaring heights created, by great myth impassioned

Patronising priests dispense 'bread and blood' of Christ
Imagined God's invented son for sin was sacrificed
Remorse with misery o'ercast, the nature of our passion
Our love and re-production they taint with a distortion
Modern myth of money magnifies our state
The new gods of profit all things permeate
No-thing can exist without, no-thing come to be
Unless the god of wealth allows by necessity
A god of loving kindness, god of all creation
Lives in glory in the head of world population
Earthquake, flood, disaster, fill the human life
Blood-filled painful death prevails from unwanted strife
The loving god from no-where back to no-where goes
Abandoning creation to wretched human woes

Popery, monarchy, imposed on squalid poverty
With monetary myth of superiority
To venerate, to eulogize, to allow to ride
With domineering despotism, undisguis-ed pride
The golden calf is worshipped in myth's masquerade
Disguised behind religion's retrograde crusade
Hoping, longing, loving, with eyes inspired to shine
By intoxication from perception of divine

Nature's golden beauty glows in every sphere
Exquisite each formation within Earth's atmosphere
Art which can reflect in truth its rich variety
With myth which can infuse, uplift us to reality
To worship at its gate with love, our minds to inspire
Catch the mystery of life, through our loves desire

In love, desires have risen, for humans to aspire
A world divested of harsh war, death from hunger dire
Where all are fed with sha-red bread, have all that is required
Where rich and poor are no more, all sheltered, cared, attired
Without crude class division, wealth made from those kept poor
Without cruel class oppression, weaponry and war
With money's wars disbanded, discarded as a shell
With human life preserv-ed, rescued from want's hell
Uplifting art inspired by nobility of mind
Knowledge, honour, dignity to civilise our kind
Burning, slaughtering weapons cease to be created
In their place the ugly face of disease defeated
Ills which will be conquered by brave humanity
Great the task and great the quest of love's humanity

PAEAN

Let the Joyful dance begin
Let Rejoicing voices ring
Celebrate Fertility
Glory in Fecundity
Reproduction's Natures message
All the rest, a mess of pottage
Out with all Hypocrisy
From Religiosity
Down with dull Morbidity
Up with Joy and Gaiety!

No more vain Imagining
Of Virgin Birth and God-fearing
How a Babe is born in Sin
How the Devil dwells within
No more false Idolatry
Of crucified Humanity
Or Irrationality
Of hoped for Immortality
Down with Lies and Piety
Up with Truth and Gaiety!

End the Immorality
Of Monarchy's Regality
And the Clear Conspiracy
Serving Class Supremacy
With its Crass Servility
And Others' sad Indignity
Out with Class Authority
Supposed Superiority
We'll have Full Equality
Prosperity and Jollity!

Our Lands arise above the Sea
One Sun warms us, Globally
End the Dark Apocalypse
Caused by the Imperialist
Profits of the Capitalist
Wars of Fascist Nationalist

Dictator's Savagery
Threat from Nuclear Weaponry
An End to their Iniquity
With INTERNATIONALITY!

See the Death of Poverty
See the rise of Liberty
See oppressed people free
From a Hated Tyranny
Down with Wars' Barbarity
Soldiers' cold Brutality
Resist their vile Atrocity
With Justified Ferocity
Fear not Death or Deity
Up with Life and Gaiety!

Sing of Mind's Nobility
Integrity, Ability
Of Moral Sensibility
Refining Sensitivity
Enlightening Sagacity
Conscious Rationality
Aspiring toward Excellence
Guided by Intelligence
Delight in our Activity
Diversity and Gaiety!

Sing of Earth's Fertility
Of Energy, Vitality
Of Virile Masculinity
Of Feminine Fecundity
From their Sacred Unity
Blossoms new Humanity
Within the Earthly Trinity
Come Feelings of Sublimity
Inspiring Creativity
With Love of Life and Gaiety!

PHOTOS OF A FAMILY (THE AUTHOR'S)
CAUGHT UP IN TWO WORLD WARS

Author's Note

I wrote many of the verses in this book as a protest against the suffering of people whose nobility of character is abused by the social system past and present, the exploitation of the the labour of the present working class and the destruction of the natural world.

The first photograph is of my parent's wedding in 1923. The two later photos of the family show the effect on my parents of the trauma of war, one in 1935 and the other in 1941. The difference is particularly clear in my father who suffered from PTSD caused by his early poverty and his experiences in the first world war where he was in charge of horses, men and equipment, experiences of which he never spoke. My mother, caring for him and the family continually through the six years of his illness, shows her endurance and dedication. The dresses in the bottom family photo were borrowed for the occasion.

The author is on the far left.

The author is on the far right.

Lightning Source UK Ltd.
Milton Keynes UK
UKHW051324021221
394947UK00001B/17